Guide for the young bride

or

Let's all just save Mankind

Dolores Howerter

AuthorHouse™
1663 Liberty Drive
Bloomington, IN 47403
www.authorhouse.com
Phone: 833-262-8899

Because of the dynamic nature of the Internet, any web addresses or links contained in this book may have changed since publication and may no longer be valid. The views expressed in this work are solely those of the author and do not necessarily reflect the views of the publisher, and the publisher hereby disclaims any responsibility for them.

This book is printed on acid-free paper.

ISBN: 978-1-4389-7344-9 (sc)
ISBN: 978-1-4685-8683-1 (e)

Print information available on the last page.

Published by AuthorHouse 07/19/2024

authorHOUSE®

Dedicated to my loving husband and the
Wonderful people that have touched my life.
They were after all, my research.

If you do not read this manual from start
To finish, I will personally hunt you down
And break your knee caps.

Till death do us part?

I guess I'll start at the beginning. I was born in 1950 and was the 4th oldest of 11 children. There were 5 girls and 6 boys, we were a Hispanic family and were raised by strict Catholic parents. Some of us today are practicing Catholics, but all of us are God fearing. I was supposed to grow up to be a nun. We lived in Denver, Colorado, a very busy and growing city. It's beautiful there, lot's to do, but there's absolutely no privacy. We were taught, both boys and girls "save sex for marriage, reserve sex for the person you intend to spend the rest of your life with." Some of us listened, some of us didn't.

I was a tom boy beating on boys, especially on my own brothers if need be, but when they got bigger I got whacked. I learned at an early age to only pick on people my own size. I never grew taller than 5'1". Mother and Daddy were always reminding us to "save sex for marriage". They didn't have to tell me, I didn't like boys anyway; I had more fun beating them at baseball, basketball, and volleyball. I'll never forget when all of us 6th grade tom boys beat the 8th grade boys at basketball. Wow! Was that power or what!

We all had our chores at home, helping with cooking, cleaning, yard work, laundry, and taking care of younger siblings. We were also taught to help the neighbors and, of course, anyone else who needed a helping hand. We still had time to hang out with our chums and get into trouble. I got into minor trouble, I assure you, with my pal, Colleen. Daddy was an electrician and mother was a housewife. She stayed home to keep an eye on us; I guess she thought it was necessary, because large families are accused of all sorts. Adultery, incest, domestic violence, murder, etc... I don't mean to sound like a suspense novel; I guess small families are accused of the exact same things. Daddy didn't want to drive us all over the place, so he bought us all bikes. Mother didn't drive.

Anyway, in the 7th grade, I went to Catholic School for one year only. One of my fondest memories of Catholic school was when one of my classmates nicknamed me "Delirious". My older siblings really loved Catholic School so they stuck with it through high school.

I went through junior high a breeze and into high school. I was no longer a tom boy. By then, you're interested in dating. When I asked my mother what I should look for in a husband she said, "Pick somebody like your Daddy". I said "Daddy is handsome". She said, "Yes, he is, but looks don't matter". I asked "They don't?" She said "No". I asked "How about money? Should I pick somebody with money?" She said, "No, money comes later, like with me and Daddy." She said, "Pick somebody that's honest, hardworking, trustworthy, patient, respectful, compassionate, intelligent, god fearing, and has a sense of humor." She went on to say that these are qualities not only your father has but qualities Jesus Christ had. My father was present when we were having this talk, and he interrupted with, "These are qualities your Mother has as well," and he said, "These are qualities you should have in yourself and qualities you should want in your spouse." Daddy also added that these are qualities you should have when you go job hunting. My Mother said "You know your father is also a self made man". I asked, "What do you mean by that?" She said, "What he accomplished he accomplished on his own. Your father has a college education because of the G. I. Bill. Then I was curious about what my mother had said about good looks not mattering. My father was an exceptionally good looking man and mother was attractive in her younger years, judging from photos I had seen of their previous years. Now, though, her looks were starting to fade. I put my father on the spot and asked him if he thought mother was very good looking. He said, "I think your Mother is the most beautiful woman in the whole world." Mother just smiled and winked at both of us.

I was starting to get noticed. I had blossomed into a beauty. You hear it all: "Beauty is only skin deep", "Beautiful women are selfish", "Beautiful Women don't know how to do anything", "Beautiful women are promiscuous". I knew none of those things were true about me. It occurred to me that beautiful women are expected to be perfect. I just wanted to be nice, because that's inner beauty.

I was still a virgin, I listened to my parents. Although at this point it was the 60's and we were having a sexual revolution in our country. You've got to understand it was more than that. It was the turbulent 60's. It was the era of long hair and hippies. I was neither. I had a mod hairstyle and dressed quite fashionably. That was another thing coming from a large family; we kids had to have jobs if we wanted spending money. I worked as a manager of a concession stand at the South Drive-in theater. I was 17 at this point. I had a lot of responsibilities; I had about 8 girls working under me. It sharpened my working skills and that was another thing Daddy said, working builds character. As manager I had to help with organizing the work shifts, I was responsible for the money in the cash register, part of the inventory, training of new personnel, and food production. Most of the concession managers in the chain of drive-ins in the Denver area were 40 years old. I also had the cleanest concession stand in the chain, quite an accomplishment for a 17 year old girl! A lot of the boys would come into the concession stand and flirt with me. Sometimes I would sit in their car after I got off of work and watch the remainder of the movie with them. I practiced my kissing techniques watching Steve McQueen and Faye Dunaway in "The Thomas Crown Affair". I was still saving my virginity at 17. I remember when some of my girlfriends were getting pregnant; "out of wedlock" they called it. That damn "sexual revolution"! I still don't understand those women that led it. Don't they know that they would have accomplished so much more if they had come up with dirty names for boys that slept around? I guess they wanted 14 year old girls coming home pregnant. What were they thinking? I don't understand anyone teaching their sons double standards.

I remember this one guy in high school, his name was Tony. He was Hispanic, gorgeous, and a jock. I kind of had a crush on him, but he didn't much care for me because I was 'too nice" and a "goofy chick". I guess that's how he described girls that said funny things. I've always had an unusual sense of humor. Anyway, in senior year Tony came to the drive –in theater and asked me to sit with him. I was kissing him and he said "you don't understand, If Connie sleeps with me, so can you". I remember saying "So what if she sleeps with you, it doesn't mean I have to." That was it! The date was over! He started mumbling under his breath, something about "if that's the way you want to play it that's fine." I had some split second thinking to do. Some boys lie about girls all the time, Maybe he was just trying to get into my pants. That's a trick the guys use. What ever, the answer was still "no!" That did it, and then he said, "O.K., can I still at least have a good night kiss?" I thought "What balls! A good night kiss!" I said, "of course not, you don't need one." That was it, he said good night and that was it. The following week at school all the boys said I was a prude; it was only the girls that were lying about me. There was another guy that used to come in the concession stand, the grandson of the owner of the theater chain. He was Anglo, handsome, rich, going to college, driving a sports car and of course, we couldn't get together after I got off work because he had a date waiting out in the drive-in lot. Then I got to know him better. He was fun, interesting, and intelligent. But I didn't want to go out with him because well, he didn't meet the criteria. He wasn't a self made man. His Aunt controlled the Family Purse strings. She told him what to wear, what to drive, and what school to attend. If we went to another drive-in, I would be suspicious when he spent all his time in the concession stand visiting with the girl behind the counter. Besides, I probably wasn't even good enough for Aunt Nancy, he would be welcome in our home, but I doubt I'd be welcome in his family's home. There was still some prejudice in Denver, not a lot, but some. So why bother with him. I heard he had a reputation with the ladies at the drive-in theater; he didn't have marriage in mind, and was just looking for someone to have sex with. Although he was still interested in me, I didn't want to have anything to do with him and eventually I never heard from him again.

I was still getting lied about in high school, mostly by the girls. Sexual lies, jealousy I suppose. Some boys lied, too. You know who men lie about? Women that do say "no", they don't' deal with rejection. I guess Beauty brings out the worst in some people, Beauty sparks desire. I couldn't handle the mobs that formed, I was only 17, so I had my hair cut very short like Twiggy's (a famous model that looked like a boy). That seemed to do the trick. No one noticed me anymore.

I graduated from Abraham Lincoln High School in 1968 and worked for a year, not knowing what I wanted to do with my life. In 1969 when I was 18, I decided to go to the Colorado Barber College and learn a trade. I was going to be a beautiful barber for a rich man and fly on his private jet all over the world. That was my fantasy. The first day of school there were about 3 girls and about 30 boys and men. All the guys were nice and starring at me. There was this big funny looking guy that came up to me and stuttered you su-r-r-e a-r-r-e b-e-u-t-t-i-f-u-l. He blushed a bright red when he said it. It was funny, men tell me I'm beautiful all the time and I don't think much of it, but when this guy said it I believed him. I suppose you can call it "Love at first fright". I asked him his name, it was Roy, and I asked if I could carpool with him. I really liked him. I found out he was 19, and he was respectful of all people. When I asked him what nationality he was, he said he was a Heinz 57, which was a combination of all sorts, but mostly German. He was the only boy that was compassionate of the Larimer Street bums that came in for a free haircut and free shave. Most of them had been drinking and wanted a quarter for a bottle of wine. Roy would help them with their coats and listen to their hard luck stories, he was kind to them. I watched Roy like a hawk. When he had a free moment he would help these drunk patrons cross the street, or go down the street, if they were lucky enough to live in a motel. Most were homeless. He often gave them a quarter and a few kind words. The other boys at the barber school had little to do with them. Some were even cruel to them.

I was still working nights and going to school during the day. It was rough. I went out with Roy on a date and you'll never believe what we did. We smoked pot. It was the first time for Roy but maybe the 6th time for me. I said" how do you like that stuff?" He said he didn't' much care for it", I said "I didn't either and I wasn't going to mess with it anymore. That marijuana sure made me feel paranoid and lost. I was really impressed that on our first date Roy didn't try to take advantage of me. It was 1969 and I was almost 19.

Colorado Barber College was super busy with clientele, co-workers, instructors, working, having fun, gossiping, studying in and out of class, and going out to lunch. I sure kept a close watch on Roy; I wanted to see what kind of guy I fell in love with. He didn't clown around as much as I did, and he never gossiped about anyone. He seemed more serious, and he sure was helpful with me with my studies. Sure enough he had all the qualities I was looking for in the man I wanted to marry. He was what you call a successful person. He didn't have extreme good looks (even though I thought he was the handsomest man I had ever seen). He didn't have any money, he just made tips from the customers, and he didn't have any power or prestige. He was just super wonderful. He bought me lunch one day, and I had him over for dinner. Mother fried the chicken and I prepared most of the remainder of the dinner. He had dinner at our home quite often after that. He felt comfortable around my family. There was absolutely no privacy in our household, with all those younger brothers and sisters, and a mother and father keeping a close watch on us! One night we decided to go out for a ride and do some smooching. We sure couldn't do it at my house. So we drove up a mountainside and wound up in this secluded area and we parked and started to kiss. I think Roy kissed me twice, we had our eyes closed and this loud voice said "You kids aren't doin' that here!" We looked up, and there was this shotgun pointed at us. We said "What?" He repeated himself, "You kids aren't doin' that here!" Roy explained that we just came up looking for privacy. The man said, "This is private property you kids better git!" Roy started up his car and we took off. It was quite frightening and comical at the same time.

Another time we went out looking for privacy we parked in the early evening, it was in a school parking lot. We had a police car follow right behind us. The policeman tapped on the car window and asked Roy if he could talk with him. The policeman wanted to know my age, he thought I looked 14, and asked to see my I.D., I was almost 19. The policeman thought Roy was too old for me. We all laughed; Roy was only 9 months older than me. There was no privacy in Denver, Colorado.

We decided to go out one night and do some drinking, another thing I had very little experience with, and I wanted to lose my virginity to him. He was reluctant at first; he said he didn't want to take advantage of a girl that had been drinking. I told him I was in love with him. I guess you can say I pretty much talked him into things. I was sure curious about sex. I was almost 19, and I was drunk. I was in love and everything was perfect. The guy I was going to have my first sexual experience with was the guy I wanted to marry. It was a painful and sloppy experience; neither of us knew what we were doing. He didn't have any experience with sex either. We experimented with sex after that a few more times. Then we decided we were in love and decided to get married. We had a lot of talking to do. Well, I didn't quite "save sex for marriage", but I did manage to "reserve sex for the one person I intended to spend the rest of my life with."

We wanted to have children right after we got married so we weren't going to use any birth control. We wanted to let it be by chance if we got pregnant. We were going to have a wedding to plan. At this point I wanted to quit the barber college anyway. Although I was creative when it came to cutting and styling hair and the studying wasn't too difficult, my hands were cracked and bleeding. I went to a couple of dermatologists; my hands were all torn up with eczema. The dermatologists said there wasn't a cure, and they advised a different line of work other than the barber business because of the harsh chemicals we used to sterilize equipment.

Roy was finished with barber school, but I wasn't, so I was going to quit school and my job and get a better paying job to pay for a wedding. Roy and I decided we were going to live in Rawlins, Wyoming, the town he was born and raised in. While I was working at my new job, which was at luggage factory, Roy went to my home and asked my parents for my hand in marriage. My older siblings were gone and all my younger brothers and sisters were there. He said it was the most embarrassing thing he has ever done! Whew! At least that hard part was over. With the Bridal Showers to go what else is there. I was waiting for the "and they lived happily ever after part". I realize now the best gift I got was "The Better Homes and Gardens Cookbook". I had some cooking skills, but that cook book taught me how to do most of my cooking. It had pictures, cooking terms, and instructions, and diagrams anyone could follow.

To get married in the Catholic Church at that time we had to have pre cana sessions. We also told both sets of parents that we weren't pregnant; we told them this because we were a teen marriage and we didn't want them having the wrong idea about us. Ours was a whirlwind romance; we met the week before Valentine's Day in February, got engaged the first week of April, and set our wedding date for August 2. The Pre Cana Sessions for marriage preparation were twice a week, for four weeks. This was to be done before the wedding.

The Pre Cana Sessions were rather interesting. We had quite a few couples attending, preparing for marriage, all different ages. Some were as young as we were and some were quite older. The very first thing we were all told was that the reason these marriage preparations are called Pre Cana is because that was the miracle Jesus Christ preformed at a wedding, by his mother's request, changing water to wine. The people leading the panel were married couples giving us the benefits of their experience, and clergyman, usually Catholic Priests. Other sessions, there were clergymen from other faiths leading us. They discussed quarrels that married couples have. They told us we were going to fight over trivial things, and we were going to fight over major things. Their exact words were "If you're going to be married for 50 years or longer, you will be." They told us to argue constructively so you won't have major fights. They told us were probably going to fight over the tube of toothpaste or weather the toilet seat should be up or down. Roy and I hadn't even had a disagreement yet, so we didn't know what they were talking about. We were just so much in love. They had a priest reminding us to keep our faith and raise our children Catholic (which we did).

I especially got a kick out of the sexuality session that told us that sex was a very important part of our marriage. They told us in the eyes of God anything that goes on between husband and wife in the bedroom (doors locked) is blessed, so long as both parties are in agreement.

I had an unusual experience a few days later. I had gone to the mall to check out a few ideas I might have for my upcoming nuptials, when I was approached by a man. He said he was a photographer and couldn't help but notice how beautiful I was and he was looking for models. I knew I was too short to be a model. So I asked him for his card and I'd get back with him at a later time, I was in kind of a hurry. Well, he didn't have cards on him, and then I asked where his equipment was. If you're looking for models at the mall wouldn't you at least be carrying a camera? He realized I was suspicious of him so he started to walk quickly away. I alerted a security guard but he got away. Later when I got home I told my mother and Roy and they both said it was a good thing I knew better than to go with him.

The wedding was beautiful, thanks to my wonderful older sister, Rosemary, who helped me plan it. I almost forgot to tell you the night before my wedding my mother sneaked into my bedroom and said "Are you sure you want to get married tomorrow, I mean the guy your marrying seems like a real nice guy and your Dad and I really like him, and we think he'll make a wonderful husband. I guess I just don't want any of my kids to get married". I said "Mother, I'm crazy about the guy, besides what are we going to do with all that cake?" She laughed, and said, "O.K., then you'd better get married. I had to giggle when I was getting ready for bed that night, I didn't have cold feet, but apparently my mother did. The wedding was great, lots of people, lots of food, booze, cake, and great presents Every where we turned the photographer was snapping pictures. During the reception my mother had a talk with me; she said "Never say no to your husband in the bedroom; never withhold sex from your husband in the bedroom, even when you're mad at him." I said "sure, mother," at that point I was so excited about sex she didn't have to tell me.

Our wedding night was fabulous! We were sound asleep when my new husband woke up with nightmares. "There's your mother!" "Cover up!" I said, "What?", "Where?", "Better not be!" He yelled, "Everybody's looking at us!", "Cover up". I looked up and said, "Calm down there's no one here." He said, "Oh, I must be having a dream. "I guess so" I said. Then he said, "Don't you have to put some curlers in your hair or something?" I said, "Why would I put curlers in my hair?" "Don't we have to take more pictures tomorrow or something?" he said. I said "No, we took all the pictures after the wedding." "OK", he said. I said "Go back to sleep." He dozed off. I didn't realize he was under so much stress, I thought it was just the bride that felt that way.

Roy passed his barber exam in Cheyenne and called a friend that lived there to come to our motel room for a visit. He brought his wife with him. They were pleasant and I liked them. When they left Roy said, "Well, we'll never see them again" I said "Why, do you say that?" "Because, I don't want to" he said. I said "why not?" Roy said "Because when he got me alone he asked if I'd like to swap wives." I said "I'm sure he was just kidding." He said "No, he was serious and I don't want anything to do with a guy that wants my wife."

When we got to Rawlins Roy had a small house to rent. The first week we were married my new husband made a kind of funny request. It was early evening. He said, "Angel, (that's what he always called me because Angeline is my middle name), do you remember that movie "the Graduate" with Dustin Hoffman and Katherine Ross, where they went to a strip show and he was really into it and she was totally disgusted? Anyway, he was starring at the stripper and said "can you do that?" I said, "What?" He said, "Yeah, that's exactly what Dustin Hoffman said in the movie to Katherine Ross, can you do that?" I said, "What are you talking about?" He said, "Well, the stripper had the tassels going in opposite directions." I said "So?" Then he said again, "Can you do that?" I said, "You mean strip, or get the tassels going in opposite directions?" He said, "Both!" "I don't know," I said, "Let's find out". I turned on the radio, "Light My Fire" by the Doors came on. He said, "That'll do nicely". So I did a real nice strip to the music. When I got most of my clothes off we taped our high school graduation tassels on my breasts, and I did, I got them going in opposite directions. When I got to the panties, Roy put them on his head and he looked so silly we both giggled and fell into each others arms. We made mad passionate love on the floor, because sex can be silly, too. The second week into our marriage Roy wanted another strip show (Roy got those often throughout our marriage).

After a couple weeks after I got to Rawlins, I got a job at the Bel Air Restaurant. I was a hostess and cashier. My boss or I should say co – owner of the restaurant, was Alex. I had a lot of people I had to answer to: waitresses, cooks, and a bartender. Alex was the best boss I ever had. He never asked his employees to do anything he wouldn't do himself. He was a self demanding person and I wanted to model myself after him.

One evening I fixed a scrumptious meat loaf dinner with mashed potatoes and gravy. After Roy ate his dinner, he said, "That was real good, but that's not the way my mother does it". He had said that the night before, when I fixed him pork chops, "That was real good, but that's not the way my mother does it". I guess I didn't like being compared to another woman. It seemed that no matter what I did Roy said, "That's real good but that's not the way my mother does it. That night I tucked him in for the night and I tucked him like he ain't never been tucked before, if you get my drift. He lay there all worn out with a smile on his face, pleased with himself, then I whispered, "I bet that's not the way your mother does it". He looked mortified but decided he was glad I wasn't quite like his mother. I had to traumatize the poor guy to make my point.

About a month after we got married my husband's old high school friend came over for a visit. He was in the service and he was home on leave. He wanted Roy to go out drinking with him. Roy asked me if he could go out with him and meet some of the guys for drinking that night and I said, "Sure, go ahead". The friend left and they were all going to meet at a local bar later on that evening. I really didn't want my husband going out drinking with the guys, but I didn't say anything because I didn't want to sound like a nag. So I came up with a plan. Just before he got ready to go out, I put on my prettiest nightgown, and touched up my make-up. When he got ready to go out the door, I said "You be sure and have a good time, but don't stay out so late because I'll be waiting up for you, and I kinda got plans for ya". Then I kissed him real seductively. He was gone about 20 minutes, just long enough to tell his friends that he'd rather stay home with his new bride. When he came home to me we snuggled a little before we made mad passionate love on the sofa. I made a point of making him feel like a King, so he'd never want to go out drinking with his buddies.

After we lived in Rawlins a couple of months we did promise my mother we'd come back to Denver for a weekend visit, plus we had to get some belated wedding gifts.

On our conversation down to Denver we discussed our family backgrounds. We both agreed there wasn't much family violence in either of our families. I had confided when we were young children we got spanked, as we got older when I called my mother a bitch I got slapped, when my sister called her that she got slapped as well, and I told him when my brother said the F word he got a good slap, too. There was always hitting among brothers and sisters, we decided that was normal. But I never saw my parents hit each other. As a matter of fact, I never saw them argue, I seldom saw them even disagree. We decided that's the kind of marriage we wanted, hardly any fighting or arguing, and definitely no name calling. I also told Roy about the incident we had at the house a year earlier when a police car drove by the house, and my brother, Ernie said, "There goes the pig". My mother flipped. She was so angry, when she gets that angry no one gets a spanking or a slap, what you get is a lecture. She rounded all of us kids together, all ages. She told us how the police are always to be respected. The police work hard to take care of everybody. They work hard at catching the criminals and taking care of good people. If you're not breaking the law you have nothing to worry about. Her final words were, "Be legal."

We had a real nice visit with my family and mother's only advice was, "if you treat your husband like a King, he will treat you like a Queen." I was already getting that treatment from my husband and I told her "I know". We started back home to Rawlins that Sunday evening.

When we started back home it was a little foggy right outside of Cheyenne. Roy wanted to show me this tree that grew out from a rock, it was considered a landmark. It looked real neat. Roy had other plans. He said it was too foggy to drive so we better wait it out for a while. It was dark out already, we were parked and well, Roy said, "Let's get in the back seat of the car and lay back and get comfortable for a couple of hours." Like I said, Roy had other plans.

I wanted to tell you about the fabulous Catholic Church I belonged to. It was St. Joseph's, and I felt very comfortable there because half of the parish was Anglo and the other half was Hispanic. I went to Sunday mass, confession, and I put money in the collection plate. That was my obligation as a Catholic.

I had finally quit my job because I was a few months pregnant. We were lucky, although we wanted children right away after we were married, we didn't actually have our first child until we were married for 20 months. When I was at the doctor's office and got the news I was pregnant, I was told that I literally glowed. We had a beautiful baby girl and nicknamed her "Princess".

The first thing we did when we had our baby and had to tend to her needs like diaper changing and getting up with her in the middle of the night, was panic. I breast fed (and planned on breast feeding all our children), so Roy didn't have to do that. It wasn't unusual, though, for him to wake up during the night when the baby woke up for a feeding. He would change the baby's diaper and put the baby at my breast, so she could nurse. It was great; he wanted me to get a full night sleep. I guess it doesn't dawn on you all the responsibilities of being a parent, until you become one. We discussed how we should forgive our parents for anything wrong they did while raising us, and how we were going to be better parents than what we had. We thought that would keep us on our toes.

Time passed and I now had a 2 year old daughter and was pregnant with my son (Who weighed 9 pounds at birth). I started getting involved in Parish duties helping with the women's group. I was very active in the church. I met wonderful women like Betsy, Lynn, Rita, Sandra, Maureen, Jean and Chris. These were creative home makers that would eventually teach me to be creative, like some crafts, and shared recipes. A few taught me how to care for plants. We did fundraising for the parish and a lot of other things. I also met a Monsignor that confused me, he wasn't always very pleasant. I thought priests were supposed to be like Jesus Christ. Jesus Christ was at least pleasant. And then I had to examine my conscience. Jesus Christ didn't make us, God did. How did God make us? He made us all different. So I didn't want to treat this Msgr. badly, even though he treated me badly.

Some of the priests I worked with over the years were different. The one I learned most of my skills from was Father Malcolm Reid. He was the one I got fatherly advice from when I needed it. With my own father so far away, and Fr. Reid here and easy to talk to, I found it more convenient and cheaper (in those days it cost a lot to talk on the phone long distance) to just visit with Fr. Reid. He used to come over once a week. I was teaching religious education (I taught different grades over the years) and we had meetings to discuss my classes, they all had different needs. Father Reid's best advice was just treating the kids the way you'd like to be treated. That's how God's going to judge us, by how we treat the people around us. Personal growth is when a person demands more from themselves than from the people around them. Often I thought these private meetings we had were better then the Sunday sermons he gave. ` Sometimes we got to talking about other things, including my in laws, which I had problems with.

One day I got a hold of a Cosmopolitan magazine that was on the counter at the grocery store and was interested in an article for the newly married bride. There was an article on how to keep your marriage always fresh, and never to stray outside your marriage, especially if you plan on staying married 50 years or longer. I was definitely interested.

The article started out with OK so every husband asks for one sooner or later we know what they're called ---- ----, you still can't say it!? We call it oral sex. Just put a little chocolate sauce and whipped cream on it and it's not that bad, maybe a little peanut butter and jelly, or maybe some nacho cheese sauce, hey, we're trying to make it as appetizing as we possibly can for this vulgar act. Maybe you can swish around some hot coffee or if he's the patriotic type you can hum the Star spangled Banner. Spit or swallow. The choice is up to you, but we recommend spitting in a sink.

Maybe we recommend a strip show for your honey. You like to dance, He likes to watch, and you have to undress eventually. That's right; he's been watching you strip every night at bedtime anyway so you might as well make it entertaining with a little background music. The article went on to say that if you have an active sex life with your husband (the sex act only takes 10 minutes) at least every day or at least every time your husband needs it (his needs will differ as time goes on) he will fall madly and deeply in love with you every time you make love. He needs to feel desirable too, so you be sure and initiate the sex act sometimes yourself. Don't discuss fantasies unless it involves him, or a famous movie star or recording artist.

Anyway, not to loose track of this article I read in Cosmopolitan it continued with ideas on role playing, costumes, wigs, etc... Some people do have fantasies about people in uniforms or repairmen, or women in position like librarians or teachers, or Catholic school girls, nurses, etc... The skies the limit, that's why they have costumes available.

The article continued with physical and emotional pain. Some people like hurling insults at each other or like hurting each others feelings. The problem with that is you can't take it back and you can cause permanent damage. Some people like causing physical pain with whips and chains or punching each other. But remember this is supposed to be behind locked doors so your children shouldn't be witnessing this. They imitate what they hear and see. I thought this was an interesting article about what some married couples do to express their love to one another. The article did say to use your own imagination and come up with some of your own ideas.

I realized then that Roy and I did have disagreements or quarrels from time to time, nothing major, but I thought it would be a good idea if we would come up with nicknames we can call each other when we were angry with each other, names our children can repeat. When Roy turned into this big ferocious animal, angry, and ready to pounce on someone I would call him "cry baby". He would turn into a little boy and whimper in my arms. In other words he was putty in my hands. When I became this big vicious witch ready to rip someone to shreds, Roy would call me "little girl". I would turn into a sobbing child in his strong arms. We were like a fairy tale like "Beauty and the Beast".

Just then the phone rang, it was my mother calling to see how we were, and of course reminding me to have sex with my husband whenever he needs it, it will inspire him. I said, "I know mother."

Roy was only a barber for six months and I was already mistaken for a hippie, by then I had long hair. Hippies were non existent in Rawlins, or Wyoming for that matter, so I didn't understand the confusion. I usually wore t-shirts and jeans because that was the dress code of Wyoming. I guess Roy and I were complete opposites but some people thought we were a cute couple. Anyway, at this point Roy was working on the Union Pacific Rail Road as a clerk. He earned less than a school teacher and we decided that I should stay home to care for our children. That's all I ever wanted to be, was a housewife. At this time we were able to purchase a very nice home because we both pinched pennies.

Father Reid came over to discuss our religion class and what I was preparing for my students. Father Reid was very consciences about his religious education program and he met with each of his instructors individually at least once a week. Anyway, Roy was trying to repair a leaky faucet in the bathroom and he was using foul language and Father Reid thought he was using foul language at me. Fr. Reid said, "You know God created man needing sex, a man can't function without it. Man needs sex to sustain; a man can't function day to day without sex. A woman on the other hand can function just as well without it. I guess you can say God played a real cruel joke when he created us. Some women just have sex to get married. Some women just have sex to have children and quit having sex when they've had their children. Why do women refuse to have sex with their husbands? Don't they realize that if they have sex with their husbands, for their husband's sake, they will learn to enjoy it? Their husbands will consider them to be the perfect wife. At this point I was pregnant with our 3rd child, (another son). I asked "Can I use birth control measures so I can continue to have sex with my husband after we have our family?" He said "The Catholic Church is against any form of birth control, I can't give you permission to use any form of it, but it's your conscience being your guide." (My husband and I had already decided or at least discussed the possibility of him having a vasectomy after we had this 3rd child). Father Reid thought my husband was angry with me for not having sex with him and I said "no, not at all, he gets all the sex he wants from me." I told Fr. Reid Roy only uses foul language when he tries to repair something. He laughed and said "I'm sorry I guess I go on and on, I thought you had a problem with your husband." I laughed and said "No, ha-ha, he's got a problem with the leaky faucet. But you know I've never heard men and women's sexuality described that way." When Fr Reid left I chewed my husband out for using foul language, period. He shouldn't be using foul language at all, not in front of me, or a priest or the children, they pick it up. I accidentally made him feel bad so I fixed him his favorite supper which was green Chile, beans, and homemade tortillas and then after we put the two children to bed we watched a little TV. Then I seduced him. I didn't want Cosmo's, Fr. Reid's, Pre Cana's and Mother's advice going to waste.

I have to tell you about my honey dew list. It's the chart I devised so I wouldn't have to nag my husband about all the chores he has to do around the house (honey do this, and honey do that). I got this sheet of paper and at the top of it I put in black marker HONEY DEW LIST. Under that, I put, I love you, and get to these at your earliest convenience. Then I listed all the chores around the house that needed to be tended to, like loose doorknobs, loose door hinges, loose or exposed wires, and leaky pipes or faucets, things I couldn't repair. This way he can get to these repairs or chores without being nagged; I put it on the calendar or if there was a bulletin board that would have worked, too.

Once we played strip poker when the electricity went out and we played by candlelight and, you guessed it, I won and it was winner's choice. All I had him do was stand on his head. I laughed when he did it in the nude. I guess my needs are simple, I just needed to giggle, and then we made love.

Sometimes he had to work later shifts and got off in the evening. He'd come home late. I was usually wiped out with taking care of the house doing laundry, folding diapers, raising children, sewing. I waited up for him and had a little something for him if he was hungry. We had our main meal before he went to work, and I usually packed him a lunch or sent him with some leftovers. So he wasn't hungry for food when he came home from work, he was usually hungry for sex. I wasn't usually in the mood for him. I remember what Cosmo said about going in different stages in your marriage. I told him I was pooped, I had a busy day. But just the same he said he was in the mood. I asked him, "Do you want a co-operative partner that tells you all the right things and is a real tigress in the sack with you or do you want some one that might just doze off and fall asleep in the middle of the sex act?" He had to think. "I guess I'm in the mood." I said "Then I'm open for business." Another time he asked for sex and I said "What is it you want, the tigress or the one that surrenders?" He said "I guess I want the tigress." I said "O.K." So I set the alarm an hour ahead to wake him up and be his tigress. I wanted to beat the kids up so they could sleep in. It was a kick! The next morning when the alarm went off he didn't want to wake up. He behaved badly, he wasn't co-operative at all, and he wanted to sleep. I laughed "you don't want to have sex?" I told him "That's how I feel when I'm not in the mood or too sleepy. So how does it feel to feel too tired to have sex?" I brought him a cup of coffee and everything. "Come on Sweetheart (that's what I always called him), let's make love." He didn't want to wake up. "Come on", I said I'm ready to be your tigress!" That did it! We had a fabulous love making session and it took longer, about 20 minutes, because we were more attentive to each other, more concerned with saying the right things to each other. Like recognizing each others good qualities and bringing them out. We had a good talk that morning and I told him I noticed that he didn't sleep as well as usual and I suspect it's because he didn't get his sex before he went to sleep. So I decided he can have his sex before and after he slept whatever his needs. Fortunately his needs weren't always like that. I also noticed that if I told him "no" to sex he was in a grumpy mood. I noticed if he had his sex he was easier to get along with; he was gentler with the children, he was probably easier to get along with at work. I decided his mind probably worked better, too. That ten minutes of sex when he needed it seemed to make him a better person. "Gee Whiz!" I thought 10 minutes did all that?

I don't know if you've guessed it, young bride, but you've been at a sexuality workshop for the young bride and of course, as usual, single girls sneaked in to get our secrets, they want to snag our men. This world is full of them, horrible women that lie about other women or sleep around to make men fall in love with them. When that doesn't work, they get themselves pregnant on purpose; to trap men into marriage. When that doesn't work they get their abortions. I suppose we have married women doing that as well.

So I challenge you women out there, which are you? Are you the honest, kind, hard working, trustworthy, compassionate woman, with a sense of humor? Do you have inner beauty? Do you have character? Which are you? The single girl (or married woman) that tries to steal boyfriends (or husbands), that lie about other women (your competition), or their sexuality (damage their reputations)? Do you lie to hide what you've done (pin your misdeeds on someone else)? Are you an idiot that just repeats what you hear? Maybe you better watch that sexual misconduct and lying altogether.

What about men that lie about their sexual conquests, do they lie to hide who they really slept with or do they lie to flatter themselves? Do they lie because they don't deal with rejection? If men and women didn't sleep around we wouldn't have this problem. The world seems to be sexually confused.

It's now 1975; my youngest child was born. We now have a girl and two boys. Roy had to take vacation time from work to care for our two oldest children while I was in the hospital. He was frantic. "How do you do it? I can't keep the house clean, I can't keep the kids clean, and I didn't have time to do laundry. I don't know if I even fed them nutritious food like you do. I know how to fry eggs and do some cooking like you showed me. But I still don't know how you do it. When are you coming home? I want you home. When is the Doctor releasing you?" He would get a sitter and come up to the hospital and visit for just a short time.

It was great getting home; everyone was anxiously waiting for the new baby. Things went back to normal. I was still involved in Parish duties and Roy and I were officers for the Union Pacific Junior Old Timers, a fun organization that kept us super busy. The J.O.T. is where we met Celsa, her husband, and many wonderful people. I really don't want to get into how we make friends and lose friends, we've all been super busy with our lives, watching life move right before our very eyes. Anyway, I wanted to be a creative homemaker. So I took courses at the extension office on cake decorating, oil painting, bread baking, and quilting. I already knew how to sew, do crafts like ceramics and macramé. I learned how to refinish woodwork. It came in handy with church bazaars, raffles, and gift giving.

Some people from the church recommended the Marriage Encounter Weekend. We made a weekend and met Father Hoodack. Marriage Encounter was a crash course in communication. It was a fabulous weekend, and of course they encouraged an active sex life for husband and wife.

One night Roy said "let's make love under the stars". We got a sleeping bag and went out in the backyard and I remembered our marriage vow from the reminder at our marriage encounter. "When two become one", that's the sex act, so God blesses our bonding. I had wished it was longer or more explicit because that's why men get married for sex. Women get married for security. Give the husband what he wants, SEX!

We had purchased a Polaroid camera (a camera that develops the picture immediately) for a church fund raiser and our personal purposes and were about to take pictures. My husband stopped and said, "Wait a minute this is no fun." "Go ahead," I said "take the picture." He said "No, go take your clothes off!" I said "What, just take the picture and see if the camera works." He said he didn't want to waste the film on a plain picture, "Just take your clothes off!" he said. I said "O.K., just a minute." I called the neighbor where the kids were playing and asked if she would keep the kids there an extra hour or so, Roy and I were working on a surprise for their Christmas and I didn't want them barging in on us. She said "Sure, fine".

We took a lot of nude photos that hour and used up a couple packages of film. I even took some photos of him. We had a lot of fun that hour or so. Afterwards we had a nice stack of dirty pictures. From time to time we would take them out and have erotic but quite often comical moments. After a few weeks of looking at these pictures and, of course, being careful where we hid them, we decided we didn't want them falling into the wrong hands (the children), so we destroyed them and threw them away.

I was still involved in parish duties, by then my youngest was almost 5 and Monsignor asked me to be in charge of the Catholic Youth Organization`. I was 30 but looked young for my age, I was often mistaken for one of the teenagers. I had a young priest assigned to work with me with the youth group. We didn't get along very well and because we were close in age we were gossiped about. Anyway, always after a hectic and frustrating youth function I came home to a loving supportive husband, who didn't mind watching his children. One night after an especially difficult outing with the young priest and the rowdy teen group I came home thourouly exhausted. After my husband and I put our kids to bed and it was our bedtime, we lied in bed. We made love with the radio on, we always liked having music on in the background when we had sex. This night my husband put me on the spot and asked "who would you leave me for?" I said "no one." He said "Aw, come on, who you would leave me for?" There was a Lionel Richie song playing on the radio and I said O.K., maybe I'd leave you for Lionel Richie. He laughed and said "O.K." We fell asleep. The next day he started following me around the house singing Lionel Richie songs in Elmer Fudd's voice. God! How I fell madly in love with my husband!

I noticed how my husband's treatment of me had changed over the years. He started by bringing me my favorite candy bar when he came home from work, or he would surprise me with a dragon for my dragon collection (Mondragon is my maiden name), or he'd come home with a beautiful nightgown . Then he would send me flowers for no special occasion, just for the "heck of it", he would say. Sometimes he would plan a get away for just the two of us, without the kids. He sure gave me the special treatment. I realized I was more than his wife , I was also his mistress. How exciting, how creative, (how naughty) what an accomplishment! Mother was right, the best thing for husband and wife was to be sexual for each other.

Young bride, I can't stress enough, the importance of being sexually available for your husband. Don't forget that's why you got married, to make each other happy, and when is he his happiest, when your making love to him. It'll all come back to you, you'll see. With your constant bonding you'll bring out the best in each other. If you withhold sex from your husband, especially for long periods of time, he may grow to resent you, and can cause friction in your relationship, and can result in marital problems, he may even fall out of love with you, you don't want that to happen. Young bride, you make sure that the honeymoon is never over!

I worked with the youth group for almost 3 years, I just couldn't work with the young priest anymore, I found him difficult to work with and teens aren't easy. I guess I decided 3 years was enough. I did get something constructive from that priest: I learned that perfection doesn't exist. Problems, none of us are without them. And nothing is better, it's just different. That priest did cause me to question my faith.

I also learned when I worked with the teenagers that most parents didn't give their children a very good sex education in the home. Not like the good one I had in my family. I found that most parents told their sons and daughters that sex is natural (instructing them to have sex), and then telling them that it's all the women's fault. What happens is you have sexually active boys and men that don't assume responsibility for their sexual behavior and blame it on the women they sleep with. They probably have many partners. When girls are taught this they, too, have many sex partners, but because it's all the women's fault it confuses them, so they lie about other women. They have to pin it on some one else, or they're passing moral judgments on women doing the same thing they're doing.

At this time we had a complete change of administration at the church, a new priest, who exploited and betrayed. I guess you can say he definitely confused me. I was wishing Fr. Reid or Fr. Hoodack was there, they would've given a sermon on jealousy being the most destructive of all human emotions. I do want it noted that although I worked with a couple of priests that caused me to question my faith, all the other priests I dealt with over the years strengthened my faith. They always inspired me to use my people skills constructively.

I do want to tell you about my only indiscretion. I was at the Keg, a local bar, one night with a friend, Gwen, (doing my research for this manual) when I was approached by a young man. He was nice; his name was Dan and he was good looking. I told him I was married and unavailable. My friend and I left. I saw him a few weeks later at the drugstore and invited him over. He followed me home. The kids were home getting ready for bed, and Dan and I were just visiting (I was doing my research). I liked him, I don't think I was calculating or had dishonest intentions; I just genuinely liked the guy. We did have a couple of alcoholic drinks and got to visiting when all of a sudden he kissed me. He surprised me. Then he kissed me again. It was a passionate kiss (I was feeling young, alive, and desirable, and I saw my husbands face); we both pulled away and said, "Wait a minute. This is wrong." It didn't go any further but it could have. He apologized saying he had never done anything like that before and I said I was just as much in the wrong and I had never done anything like that either. He said, "you're beautiful, what can I say". I said "You're a real nice guy, which was the attraction, if I was a few years younger, and single, I'd be wanting to run off with you" We both laughed and he left.

When my husband got home during the early morning hours that next day, I snuggled up to him and felt guilty. It ate at me that day what I had done or what it could have been, and I told him about it. He was hurt that I would participate, but I told him he should be used to men kissing me all the time. When we'd go out a lot of the older gentlemen would kiss me (fatherly kisses, I assure you), as would a couple of the fresher younger men. I guess they were comfortable kissing their beauty queen. I guess all the other kisses were no big deal. I reminded my husband that ever since I was 14, I attracted the opposite sex (pig sweat, they call it) but when I reached 16 I turned into a beauty and I heard all the lines. When I got older men started offering me gifts or even trips for sex. I never took them up on it. I told my husband the attraction to this guy was the fact that he did remind me of my husband. He didn't offer me power, prestige, money, or good looks; he was just an ordinary guy like my husband. He was a nice honest guy and he didn't take advantage of a weak moment, that's what made him special. He was just like my husband. When I told my husband this he wasn't so hurt anymore. I did promise to spend the rest of my life making it up to him, and I did offer to bend over so he can give me a quick kick in the rear. He didn't, he laughed and he forgave me, and we both felt better. Then we made love, the best way for us to bond. I had my lesson in infidelity and I gotta say, "It sure scared the hell out of me".

I was at a local exercise place working out when these two women I recognized waved me over. One of the women said that her husband was mad at her and she wanted to get back in his good graces. What should she do? I said she should "Screw his lights out! That always works, that's what makes your husband happy doesn't it?" She said "Yes, it does, but you don't understand, he hit me". I said "What! Wait a minute that does shed a different light on things." Then I asked, "Did you hit him first?" She said, "Yes, I did." The other woman present said, "It doesn't matter". I said, "It does matter, you never start with the hitting, violence is never good especially in a marriage." The woman that got hit admitted that it was wrong and things got out of hand. I asked her, "What do you want to do? Do you want to divorce and go your separate ways or do you want to stay married and make the best of it?" She said she loved her husband and wanted to make her marriage work. I said "Then screw his lights out". The other woman said, "Isn't that using sex as a weapon?" I said, "Yeah, it is, so you make sure he doesn't know what hit him." We all giggled. The other woman said "Maybe, she just needs to talk to him." I said, "Maybe she'll say all the wrong things and they'll start fighting again." I said, "Why don't you just try it? What have you got to lose? Just screw his lights out, you be sure and say all the right things, you want to remind him why he married you in the first place." She said she'd do it. She came back the next day and said it worked. I was delighted. I gave her her own private sexuality workshop, pretty much what I've included in these pages. I wanted her to understand that all a husband wants from his wife is a little sugar. When she moved away about 2 months later she said she appreciated my help and it made a big difference in her marriage. She said, "You don't understand, I am so grateful." I said, "You don't understand, just give your husband that 10 minutes of sex whenever he needs it, and you'll make sure he's the grateful one." She said "Gotchya!"

A place I liked going for coffee every morning at 6 a.m. was the Rifleman Club Bar, owned by Frank and Patsy, a couple I love like my own parents. One morning there was a policeman in there getting a cup of coffee, and I asked about the prostitution problem. I asked, "Who are the number one clients of prostitutes?" He said "married men". I asked, "What sex act are they performing?" He said, "Blow jobs". I asked, "Are these prostitutes beautiful?" He said "No". That's what I hated about the movie, "Pretty Woman"; it gave women the wrong idea about sex. What do you say, married women? Let's say we put prostitutes out of business. TEND TO YOUR WIFELY DUTIES!

Everything took a toll on me; I felt sometimes that I had the weight of the world on my shoulders. Everyone was making demands on me; I was still involved in parish duties, working on two quilts at the same time, mother duties and a wonderful forgiving husband that makes demands on me, too. I questioned my faith in myself because I always demanded perfection from myself and I felt I failed. The one person I never lost faith in was my husband, he's the one person I can count on, the one person I can believe in. He's the one I always cling to. I did eventually snap out of it.

I won't bore you with the gory details of raising children. One person told me when your child is born until they reach about 13 years old, you'd do anything to protect them, then after that all you do is protect them from yourself, in other words, when they reach puberty you want to kill them yourself.

I was still a homemaker working on family quilts, embroidery, and a lot of macramé. In addition to parish duties I was a Cub Scout den mother and belonged to Big Brothers/Big Sisters. Plus I was going through this phase of doing a lot of experimenting in the kitchen, I just always kept myself always super busy.

You start early with your children to keep their noses clean, be legal, obey the law, follow the 10 commandments and pray often. God listens. You try to set a good example because the home is where they do most of their learning. I was always aware that I wasn't the only influence they had in their lives. I tried to teach them that everyone had good qualities and bad qualities, including your own parents, teachers, bosses, friends, people you admire or people you don't even like, and people in position or power, for that matter. I told them to imitate their good qualities not their bad ones.

You have to answer for what you do. In other words you have to assume responsibility for your own actions. You have to answer to your parents, the law and other authority figures, but especially you have to answer to God. His law is the one you have to abide by.

You give to your children; you give, give, and give. Sometimes they learn to give, too. Sometimes, they just learn to take. We tried to teach our children that everyday is Christmas, and that you give of yourself and you won't necessarily be thanked, but that's O.K. because that's the way Jesus Christ and Santa Claus give of themselves.

Always when my husband would come home from work, I would tell him what his children were up to. If they needed a talking to by their father, he gave them a talk. I usually handled things pretty well, at this time in our lives my husband was an engineer with the railroad and he was home a day and gone a day. I didn't keep secrets from my husband. All three of our children were teenagers at the same time; I always made the joke that I was back to my sleepless nights. We all pretty much got along. Anytime there are two people involved you've got power plays going on (who gets to be the boss), you should try to work as a team. We didn't place blame either, that was the immature thing to do, and we simply solved the problem.

I always tried to instill that we all had to answer to God for what we've done; it pretty much kept all of us on the straight and narrow. We've all had scrapes with the law excluding my husband. He's the only one that seems to behave himself. In the end we've had communication in our family as individuals, as a team (husband and wife, king and queen), or as a group. We have unconditional love for one another. Whatever our shortcomings, we would still love each other, we would forgive each other, we would stay family. That's what Jesus Christ would do. That's also what God would do. God made us to be different, to love, and forgive. Forgive, forget, and start all over again, that's what marriage and life is all about.

Favorite Recipes

11O Year Old Pie Crust

2 ½ c. flour　　　　　1 egg (beaten)
1 tsp. salt　　　　　　1 Tbl. vinegar
l c. shortening　　　　¼ c. milk

Cut in flour, salt and shortening until crumbly. Mix together the following egg, vinegar, and milk and add to the first mixture. This makes enough dough for a two crust and a single pie crust. This pie dough freezes well, is very easy to make and never fails to be very flaky.

Potato Bread

2 2/3 cups tepid water　　　　　　6 ½ cups flour
3 tablespoons sugar　　　　　　　4 tablespoons nonfat dry milk
4 teaspoons active dry yeast　　　　4 tablespoons vegetable or olive oil
1 ½ cups instant mashed potato flakes　　2 teaspoons salt

In a large bowl mix water, sugar, yeast, and instant potato flakes together. Let stand 5 minutes. Mix in flour, dry milk, oil, and salt. Knead or mix in heavy-duty standing mixer, or by hand, 10 minutes. Press dough into two greased 4 ½ x 8 ½ inch bread pans. Cover and let rise, until double. Bake at 350 degrees for 30 minutes
　　　(tepid means room temperature, a bit cooler than lukewarm).

Tortillas

3 cups flour
3 teasp. Salt
5 teasp. Baking powder
3 tbl. Shortening
1 ½ cups hot water

mix dry ingredients, cut in shortening with fingertips , mixing well, add water slowly, mix a little at a time. Eventually mix all flour with water, if too sticky add a little more flour and knead for four minutes, until it's a smooth dough. Pinch off about 12 golf ball size balls and set covered for 10 minutes (needs to rest). Heat griddle, just below medium heat. Roll out tortillas with rolling pin and just a little flour to avoid sticking. Cook on griddle about 15 seconds on each side (keep an eye on them). They must cool slowly, between two kitchen towels.

Cinnamon Rolls

½ cup milk   ½ cup sugar
1 ½ teasp. Salt   ½ stick margarine
½ cup tepid water   2 packages of yeast
2 eggs beaten   4 to 4 ½ cups of flour

Scald milk, stir in sugar, salt and margarine, cool to tepid temperature. Dissolve yeast in tepid water, stir in milk and egg mixture, add half of the flour, beat until smooth, add the remaining flour gradually. Knead until smooth. Place in greased bowl, cover, let rise until double. Punch down and roll out to 10x15 inches, spread 3 tablespoons of margarine evenly on dough, sprinkle 2 ½ teaspoons of cinnamon evenly, sprinkle ½ cup of brown sugar, and then sprinkle ½ cup of chopped pecans or raisins. Take the widest (15 inch) side and roll up like jelly roll. Slice off 12 equal slices and place in greased 9x12 pan or two round cake pans. Cover, Rise until double, bake at 350 degrees for 15 to17 minutes.

Cool a little and cover with glaze:
1 1/2 c. powder sugar, 1 Tablespoon of margarine and 2 Tablespoons of water.

Helpful Hint: A quick way to rise bread dough is to preheat the oven to 200 degrees, but be sure and turn it off! Put your covered bowl of dough or whatever you want to rise in the heated oven, and place a small saucepan of water that has been brought to a boil in the oven with it (to keep it moist). This will cut your rising time in half.

Toffee

½ lb. Butter (not margarine)
1 cup sugar
2 Tbls. Water
1 cup chopped pecans
12 oz. semi-sweet chocolate chips

In heavy saucepan melt down butter, at medium heat, add sugar and water. Keep stirring, and cook until a medium caramel color, turn off heat, add ½ cup chopped pecans, stir quickly, spread in 9x12 pan, work quickly because toffee will start to set. When spread as evenly as possible, sprinkle chocolate morsels evenly on top and let set until melted, use knife to spread melted chocolate evenly, and sprinkle with ½ chopped pecans. Let cool about four hours. Cut or break in pieces.

Creamy Fudge

3 cups sugar
1 cup butter or margarine
1 1/3 cup evaporated milk (2 5 oz. cans)
1 13 oz. jar marshmallow cream

24 oz. semi-sweet chocolate chips
1 teaspoon vanilla
3 cups chopped nuts

Spray 9x12 pan. In heavy 3 qrt. Pan, at medium heat, place sugar, butter, milk, and marshmallow cream. Heat to boil, boil 5 minutes, stirring constantly. Take off heat and add chocolate chips and vanilla, stir until melted, add nuts, stir. Spread in prepared pan and refrigerate overnight.

Waldorf Salad

2 cups diced apple
1 cup 1 inch celery sticks
½ cup broken walnuts
¼ cup mayonnaise
1 tablespoon sugar
½ teaspoon lemon juice
    dash of salt
½ cup whipping cream, whipped

Combine apple, celery, and nuts. Blend mayonnaise, sugar, lemon juice, and salt. Fold in whipped cream; fold into apple mixture; chill. Makes 4 to 6 servings.

Veggie Pizza (2 9x 12 pans)

2 pkg 8 crescent rolls. Press each pkg. to bottom of each pan (ungreased) Bake at 350 degrees 8 minutes, brown and cool.
Mix: ¾ cup mayonnaise
        ½ cup sour cream
        2 8 oz. pkg cream cheese
        1 envelope Ranch Salad Dressing Mix

Cream together well. Makes two cups. Spread 1 cup mixture on each crust, top with chopped vegetables, broccoli, cauliflower, shredded carrots, sliced cucumber, any chopped veggie you like, shredded cheese if you like, too. Keep refrigerated and covered.

Clam Chowder

2 cans chopped clams (6 oz. size or larger if desired)
1 cup chopped onions
1 cup diced celery
3 cups diced potatoes
¾ cup butter or margarine
¾ cup flour
1 ½ teaspoons salt
1 teaspoon sugar
1 quart milk

Cook vegetables in juice drained from clams plus enough water to cover. Cook about 20-25 minutes, or until vegetables are tender. Melt butter or margarine, add flour, salt and sugar. Mix well. Add milk gradually. Cook over medium heat until slightly thickened, stirring constantly. Add to vegetables (do not drain) and simmer a few more minutes. Add clams, heat through. Serve hot with homemade bread and butter.

Alfredo Sauce

In saucepan, put one egg yolk, break it up and stir in one cup of heavy whipping cream. Turn on to medium heat. This will thicken slightly, add one cup of grated Parmesan cheese and a dash of nutmeg. Pour this over a pound of cooked pasta (I recommend Grandma's Noodles) that have been buttered with a stick of butter. You can add cooked chicken, cooked shrimp, or crabmeat.

Rice and Broccoli Casserole (9x9 pan)

2 cups cooked rice (1 1/3 cups boiling water and 1 1/3 cups minute rice make 2 cups rice)
3 Tbls. Butter or margarine
10 oz. frozen chopped broccoli (thawed)
1 can cream of chicken soup
1 soup can of milk
1 small jar (8 oz.) Cheez Whiz
2 Tbls. Ortega chopped jalapeno
1 cup chopped onion
1 cup chopped celery
salt and pepper

Saute onions and celery in butter. Add soup and milk to onions and celery. Add cheese whiz, simmer. Add thawed broccoli, chopped jalapeno, cooked rice and seasoning, simmer for five minutes. Bake in 9x9 pan, 350 degrees for 30-40 minutes. Can be made ahead of time.

Potato Salad

5 medium potatoes, boiled for 25 minutes (until tender) and cooled
5 eggs, boiled for 15 minutes and cooled, and peeled
2 slices onion, chopped
2 tablespoons sweet pickle relish
1 ½ teaspoons salt
1 cup mayonnaise
1 squirt mustard

If you scrub your potatoes well before you boil them, you won't need to peel them for this salad. Chop up cooled potatoes and eggs, add onions and sprinkle with salt, add relish. In separate bowl mix mayonnaise and mustard and mix well into other ingredients. Keep refrigerated.
Variation: Try substituting some or all of the mayonnaise with creamy Italian salad dressing (omit mustard), you might like it.

Cheesy Scalloped Potatoes (9x9 pan)

6 medium potatoes
½ onion chopped
6 Tablespoons margarine
4 tablespoons flour
3 cups milk
1 ½ teaspoons salt
8 slices American Cheese

In saucepan, medium heat, melt butter, add flour, stir in milk. Stirring occasionally add salt and cheese. While this thickens, scrub (again, if you scrub your potatoes well, you don't have to peel them) and slice potatoes and arrange in 9x9 sprayed pan with chopped onions. When sauce thickens, pour over potatoes, and sprinkle shredded cheese on top. Cover with foil and bake for two hours at 350 degrees, uncover the last ½ hour.

B B Q Country Style Pork Ribs (9x12 pan)

6 pounds country style pork ribs
½ large onion chopped
4 cups ketchup
2/3 cup brown sugar
1/3 cup lemon juice
2 large squirts mustard
1 teaspoon crushed red chile pepper (optional, this makes the sauce spicey)

Place pork ribs in pan, cook in oven at 500 degrees for one hour, draining grease, and turning half-way through, and draining again when hour is up. While meat is browning in oven make sauce: Sauté chopped onion in saucepan that has been sprayed, add all the next ingredients, simmer while meat is browning. When meat is finished browning and grease drained, pour sauce over it, cover with foil. Bake at 325 degrees for 2 hours, take cover off last 20 minutes.

Chile with Beans (16 qrt. Pot)

2 lbs bag kidney beans
2 lbs bag pinto beans
2 lg onions chopped
4 bell peppers, chopped
8 lbs hamburger
2 28 oz cans crushed tomatoes
1 - 1½ tablespoons crushed red chile pepper
4 tablespoons red mild chile powder
3 tablespoons salt
2½ tablespoons garlic powder

Clean and rinse beans in colander, place in 16 qrt. Pot with about ¾ full of water, cook beans. They take about 4 hours to cook so about halfway through, in another large pot, cook hamburger, drain fat and add the rest of the ingredients. Add to cooked beans and simmer.

Enchilada Casserole (2 9x12 pans)

3 lbs ground chuck
¾ cup canola oil
5 heaping tablespoons flour
1 tablespoon garlic powder
1 tablespoon salt
2 heaping tablespoons red chile powder
1 level tablespoon red crushed chile pepper
6 cups water
1 ½ lbs sharp cheese, shred
1 ½ lbs American cheese, shred
18-20 corn tortillas

Crumble and fry ground chuck, add oil, flour, stir in seasonings and chiles add water, this will thicken. Put meat sauce in bottom of each pan, put a layer of corn tortillas, and pour and spread sauce, sprinkle with chopped onions and sprinkle with both cheeses. Put another layer of tortillas, sauce, onions, and cheeses. Bake at 350 degrees for 40 minutes. You can cover this with foil and it freezes very well.

Fried Chicken

Moisten chicken pieces with water or milk (or buttermilk for a thicker coating) before dredging with flour that has been seasoned with salt and pepper. Deep fry in a Presto deep fat fryer in canola oil at 400 degrees for 15 minutes, let cool 5 minutes. Cool oil and pour into old coffee can with cover so it can be used over again.

Manicotti With Cheese Filling

8 oz. pkg American Beauty Manicotti
8 oz. (2 cups shredded mozzarella cheese)
2 (12 oz.) cartons cream cottage cheese
2 eggs slightly beaten
½ cup dry bread crumbs
½ cup grated parmesan cheese
2 tablespoons chopped parsley, if desired
1 teaspoon sugar
½ teaspoon salt
¼ teaspoon pepper
1 qrt. (4 cups) meat sauce (recipe below)
¼ cup grated parmesan cheese

Meat sauce: fry and crumble 1 lb. Italian sausage with chopped onion. Drain fat, add 2 6 oz. cans tomato paste, 4 cans water, salt, pepper, oregano to taste, simmer while preparing manicotti.

Heat oven to 350 degrees, cook manicotti to desired doneness as directed on the package.
In large bowl combine remaining ingredients except meat sauce and ¼ cup parmesan cheese. Stuff each cooked manicotti with about 1/3 cup filling. Spread 2 cups meat sauce on bottom of 9x12 pan. Place each filled manicotti in single layer over sauce. Pour remaining sauce over top. Cover and bake at 350 degrees for 40-45 minutes. Let stand 5-10 minutes before serving. Sprinkle with ¼ cup parmesan cheese. 7 servings

Lasagna (makes 2 9x12 pans)

Fry: 3 lbs. hot Italian sausage (crumble), drain fat
Add: ½ chopped onion, continue to fry add salt, pepper, and about 2 teaspoons of garlic powder.
Add: 5 6 oz. cans tomato paste
10 cans of water
3 pinches thyme
4 tablespoons oregano powder
2 bay leaves
Mix well, and simmer over low heat for four hours.
Boil: 2 8 oz. pkg lasagna noodles until tender
Slice: 2 lbs mozzarella cheese
Mix: 2 lbs cottage cheese
  1 cup sour cream
    4 Tablespoons parsley flakes
    2 Tablespoons chopped chives
    garlic powder

Lightly oil two 9x12 pans. First put about 4 Tbls. Sauce on bottom of pans. Then begin with !/4 noodles, then spread ¼ cottage cheese mixture over noodles as evenly as possible. Then distribute ¼ of sliced mozzarella cheese, and then spread ¼ of meat sauce, do this for both pans. Repeat, ending with meat sauce. Top with sprinkling ½ cup grated Parmesan cheese on each pan. Bake at 375 degrees for 40 minutes, let stand for 10 minutes before serving. This can be covered with foil and frozen. Each pan serves eight.

 Tip: For those that prefer a spicey Lasgna,
   you can add a teaspoon of crushed red
   chile pepper to the sauce before you
   simmer for four hours.

Spaghetti Sauce with Meat Balls

1 large can tomato juice
1 large can crushed tomatoes
2 6 oz. cans tomato paste
4 bay leaves
large pinch sweet basil
large pinch of Rosemary
1 teaspoon oregano powder
1 tablespoon salt
1 tablespoon garlic powder
1 pkg sliced mushroom (optional)

Mix all above ingredients in large pot on low heat.

Meat Balls: In large mixing bowl you mix 3 lbs. hamburger, 2 lbs. Italian sausage, 1 chopped on-ion, ½ sleeve of crushed saltine crackers, 2 beaten eggs, and 1 teaspoon of crushed red chile pep-per (optional). Form into balls the size you want, and brown them in skillet that has been sprayed. When brown on both sides put them in simmering meat sauce and simmer a couple of hours. Spoon over cooked spaghetti and sprinkle grated parmesan cheese.

Spaghetti Sauce with Meat Balls (16 qrt pot)

1   46 oz can tomato juice
5   28 oz cans crushed tomatoes
4   12 oz cans tomato paste
1 chopped onion
2 pkgs sliced mushrooms
2 tablespoons garlic powder
6 bay leaves
1 tablespoon sweet basil
1 tablespoon Rosemary
2 tablespoons oregano
2 ½ Tablespoons salt
1 teaspoon crushed red chile pepper (optional)
Put all of the above ingredients in large 16 qrt pot and put at low heat.

Meat Balls: 3 lbs. Italian sausage
                   5 lbs. hamburger
                   1 onion, chopped
                   2 sleeves of saltine crackers, crushed
                   7 eggs, beaten
                   2 tablespoons salt
                   2 tablespoons garlic powder
                   1 tablespoon of crushed red chile pepper (optional)

Mix all ingredients in extra large bowl and form into balls. Brown on each side in skillet that has been sprayed with cooking spray. Put browned meatballs in simmering meat sauce and cook at low simmer for a couple of hours.

Green Chile (large pot)

8 lbs. of pork loin cut in 3 or 4 pieces, simmer in 7 qrts of water for 40 minutes. Save water. Cool and cut up add to water and add:

2 large cans diced tomatoes
6 4 oz. cans Ortega diced jalapenos (or dice 8-10 fresh jalapenos)
7 7 oz. cans Ortega chopped green chiles
(or fresh green chiles that have been roasted and peeled)
4 chopped Habanero peppers (optional, these are very, very hot)
2 ½ Tablespoons salt
2 Tablespoons garlic powder

In large skillet at medium heat, heat 2 ½ cups of canola oil and add 4 cups of flour, stirring constantly, as not to scorch, when it turns the color of a penny add 1 large chopped onion, stir to sauté, when sautéed add to the water with the other ingredients. Simmer 1 Hour.

Helpful hint: If chile is too thick, add a little more water; if chile is too thin make a little more oil and flour, and darken, and add to Chile.

Rocky Road Buttermilk Cake

2 cups sifted flour	½ cup canola oil
¼ teaspoon salt	½ cup butter or margarine
1 ¾ cup sugar	½ cup buttermilk
4 tablespoons cocoa	1 teaspoon soda
1 cup cold water	2 eggs (beaten)

In 2 qrt bowl mix flour, salt, sugar and cocoa. In small pan melt butter, add oil and water. Bring to a boil. Pour over dry ingredients and beat with mixer until creamy. Add buttermilk, soda and eggs. Beat well. Bake in greased 11x16 pan, at 400 degrees, 18-20 minutes.

Icing:	½ cup butter or margarine	1 lb.(3 ¾ cups) powder sugar
	¼ cup cocoa	1 cup chopped nuts
	6 tablespoons buttermilk	½ teaspoon vanilla

Combine butter or margarine, cocoa, buttermilk, bring to boil, remove from heat and add remaining ingredients stir well. Spread on top of cake while hot.

A FEW AFTER THOUGHTS FROM THE AUTHOR

Young bride, I included some of my favorite recipes. Some are large quantity. There's a reason for my madness. I always figured if you're going to make a big mess in the kitchen, make a bigger one all at once. I would buy extra 9x9 or 9x12 pans at garage sales and make extra casseroles, or I would save all my large margarine tubs and freeze extra spaghetti sauce, Chile or green Chile. We purchased a freezer early in our marriage for this purpose, I also shopped grocery specials and froze extra meats when they would go on sale, or there would be days I would do extra baking (breads and rolls) and these, too, went in the freezer. That way first thing in the morning, I would take something out of the freezer for dinner. This way when I was busy throughout the day going to the gym, tackling kids, and doing volunteer work (saving mankind), my family always had a home cooked meal everyday. Fast food was unheard of in our household, and we went out to dinner, rarely.

I mentioned garage sales earlier. I gotta tell you that's where I found some of my greatest treasures. When we were a newly married couple starting out and we needed to furnish our home, because the down payment took all our savings, we found almost new furniture at garage sales. I found an old dining room set at a garage sale and we spent the summer refinishing it in the garage. You have fun with projects like that, and you can save a lot of money.

You can find nice clothing if you don't mind hand me downs for your small children (the kids won't mind), at the garage sales. Books are so cheap if you like to do a lot of reading. You can find new and almost new items at garage sales.

Estate sales also have a lot of interesting things, you can find a set of china or old records (something I still look for). You can find antiques and all sorts of interesting things. I just wanted to share some extra tips on saving money.

Dolores and her little "Princess"
in their look a like dresses Dolores made in 1973.

Dolores in 1982 when she just finished
with the C.Y.O. and started her research.

Dolores and Roy Howerter A.K.A. "Beauty and the Beast"
have been honeymooning for 40 years.

They have 3 grown children and 6 grandchildren.

Printed in the United States
by Baker & Taylor Publisher Services